THE ANIMAL KINGDOM

The INSECT World

KEITH PORTER

Editorial planning
Jollands Editions

M MACMILLAN EDUCATION

© Macmillan Education Limited 1986
© BLA Publishing Limited 1986

All rights reserved. No reproduction, copy or transmission of this publication may be made without written permission.

No paragraph of this publication may be reproduced, copied or transmitted save with written permission or in accordance with the provisions of the Copyright Act 1956 (as amended).

Any person who does any unauthorised act in relation to this publication may be liable to criminal prosecution and civil claims for damages.

First published 1986

Published by
MACMILLAN EDUCATION LTD
Houndmills, Basingstoke, Hampshire RG21 2XS
and London
Companies and representatives
throughout the world

Designed and produced by BLA Publishing Limited,
Swan Court, East Grinstead, Sussex, England.

Also in LONDON · HONG KONG · TAIPEI · SINGAPORE · NEW YORK

A Ling Kee Company

Illustrations by Steve Lings/Linden Artists, Fiona Fordyce and BLA Publishing Limited
Colour origination by Chris Willcock Reproductions
Printed in Italy by G. Canale & C. S.p.A. — Torino

British Library Cataloguing in Publication Data

Porter, Keith
  The insect world. — (Macmillan world library.
  The animal kingdom)
  1. Insects — Juvenile literature
  I. Title
  595.7   QL467.2

ISBN 0-333-40933-7

Acknowledgements

The Publishers wish to thank the following organizations for their invaluable assistance in the preparation of this book.

Rentokil
Shell

Photographic credits

t = top b = bottom l = left r = right

cover: Anthony Bannister/NHPA

4 ZEFA; 5t Stephen Dalton/NHPA; 5b, 7 Aquila; 9 Reproduced by permission of the Director, British Geological Survey (NERC); 11t Stephen Dalton/NHPA; 11b, 12 Aquila; 13t A Shell photograph; 13b Biophoto Associates/NHPA; 15t, 15b Stephen Dalton/NHPA; 16 Biophoto Associates/NHPA; 17 Anthony Bannister/NHPA; 18 Biophoto Associates/NHPA; 19 Keith Porter; 21t A Shell photograph; 21b Stephen Dalton/NHPA; 22 Anthony Bannister/NHPA; 23 A Shell photograph; 24 Ivan Polunin/NHPA; 25 Anthony Bannister/NHPA; 26, 27t Stephen Dalton/NHPA; 27b, 28/29 Aquila; 29b James Carmichael/NHPA; 30 Anthony Bannister/NHPA; 31 ZEFA; 32 Keith Porter; 33 G.J. Cambridge/NHPA; 34, 35t Anthony Bannister/NHPA; 35b Stephen Dalton/NHPA; 37 Anthony Bannister/NHPA; 38 Ivan Polunin/NHPA; 39 Aquila; 40b Stephen Dalton/NHPA; 40/41, 41b Rentokil; 42t Aquila; 42b A Shell photograph; 43 Anthony Bannister/NHPA; 44 Aquila; 45t Stephen Dalton/NHPA; 45b NHPA

Note to the reader
In this book there are some words in the text which are printed in **bold** type. This shows that the word is listed in the glossary on page 46. The glossary gives a brief explanation of words which may be new to you.

Contents

Introduction	4	Butterflies and moths	28
What is an insect?	6	Crickets and their relatives	30
Before the dinosaurs	8	One pair of wings	32
Thousands of types	10	Bugs and beetles	34
Insect skeletons	12	Water insects	36
How insects move	14	Unusual insects	38
Seeing and feeling	16	Insects in our homes	40
Breathing and feeding	18	Insects that cause harm	42
A life cycle	20	How insects help us	44
Insects everywhere	22		
Insect builders	24	Glossary	46
Bees and wasps	26	Index	48

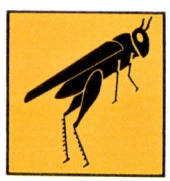

Introduction

How much do you know about insects? Most of us only notice large insects and those that bite or sting. The rest we ignore as small, black creepy-crawlies. In fact, the insect world is full of surprises.

Like all animals, each insect does a job. Without them our world would be very different.

A tiny world

Insects live in a strange world. A slight breeze can blow them away. Grass blades become tree trunks. Pebbles are like mountains. Even raindrops turn into deadly pools.

On a summer day the ground can be very hot. Even so, every morning a thin layer of ice covers the same ground. We do not see or feel these things. We stand well above the world of the insect. Our warm bodies protect us from the cold. The body of an insect does not stay warm like ours. It cools down during the cold night.

Shapes for life

Insects cope with their world in many ways. Millions of years of living has shaped each type of insect. Some are long and thin and live in tunnels. Others are shaped for flying.

No two types live in exactly the same place. Some insects survive where no other animals can. Young midges live in hot springs. They can stand temperatures that would fry other animals. One kind of fly even breeds in pools of oil.

▼ You can find insects almost anywhere on Earth. Young midges live at temperatures up to 40°C in these hot springs of Yellowstone Park, Wyoming, USA.

Introduction

Most insects live on or near plants. They are shaped and coloured to look like parts of plants. Life is a constant battle for them. There are so many other animals who want to eat them.

Insect skills

Insects make good use of their tiny world. Every insect has its own special skills. They use their feet and mouths as tools. Some have mouths which chisel into wood. Others use their jaws as tiny scissors.

Insects called termites live in huge nests. Each type of termite has a different shape and skill. They have soldiers, nurses, food gatherers and queens. The soldiers have huge jaws and the queens have fat bodies full of eggs.

Many insects make their own building materials. Some use silk to make their homes. Bees use wax to make perfect shaped nests. Even humans make use of some insect skills. Silk thread and wax for candles both come from insects.

▲ Honeybees are expert builders. These food stores would put many human builders to shame.

▼ Leaf-cutter ants cut and gather leaves. Then they eat a fungus that grows on the leaves.

What is an insect?

All large animals, such as fish, birds, and humans, have a bony **skeleton** and a soft skin. This helps to form the shape of the animal. The bodies of insects are different. They have a hard skin called an **exoskeleton**. It protects and shapes the insect.

The insect skin stops its body from drying out. There are other small animals that have exoskeletons. Unlike insects, some of them dry out quickly. One is the woodlouse, it has to live in a damp place. If it did not, it would die.

Animals in groups

All animals belong to groups. Insects belong to the biggest group, called the **arthropods**. Arthropod is a Greek word which means 'jointed-feet'. All the group have legs which are like small pieces of tubing stuck together. The legs can bend where the tubes join.

Insects are the only arthropods to have six legs. Others in the group have eight legs and often many more. The spiders, with eight legs, are most like the insects. Most insects also have wings.

All insects have a body made up of three main parts. These are the head, a **thorax** which is in the middle, and a 'tail' or **abdomen**.

▼ The arthropod group is split into four parts, one of which includes all insects.

ARTHROPODS

- Trilobita (e.g. trilobite)
- Crustacea (e.g. shrimp)
- Chelicerata (e.g. spider)
- Uniramia
  - Hexapoda (e.g. insects)
    - Winged insects (e.g. fly)
    - Wingless insects (e.g. silverfish)
  - Peripatus (e.g. velvet worm)
  - Myriapoda (e.g. centipede)

What is an insect?

▲ All insects have three main parts. The head is the insect's control centre. The thorax is the power plant. The abdomen holds the stomach.

Keeping warm

Insects are **cold-blooded** animals. This means that they warm up or cool down as the weather changes. Many animals, like humans, are **warm-blooded**. We keep our bodies at a steady heat by using food as fuel.

Insects must be warm enough to be able to fly or move quickly. One way of getting warm is to sunbathe. Many insects are dark in colour to help them soak up heat from the sun. Dark colours do this better than pale colours.

Many insects pass the winter by keeping still, or **hibernating**. This is their way of living through cold weather. Insects which live in warm parts of the world are active all year. Their problem may be that they get too hot. Desert insects often have long legs to keep their bodies off the hot sand.

▶ In the winter it is too cold for many insects to lead an active life. These seven-spot ladybirds have huddled together and will not become active again until the weather is warm.

7

Before the dinosaurs

Insects have lived on Earth for a very long time. The remains, or **fossils**, of the very first insects are found in rocks. They are over 350 million years old.

The first insects

The first insects had no wings. Their bodies were made up of a head, thorax, and abdomen. They probably fed on dead bits of plants. Fossils of later insects show that some grew small bumps on their thorax. These are thought to be the start of wings and helped the insects to glide.

Three hundred million years ago the world was covered by warm swamps full of plants. These made a good home for all types of insect.

Most of these insect types had wings. Some of them looked like dragonflies. They had wings up to 75 cm across. These monster insects are not found today. They did, however, give rise to modern dragonflies.

▼ Insects have been flying on Earth for some 300 million years. Fossils of early insects tell us that some were huge. Ones that looked like this had wingspans the length of an adult human's arm.

Before the dinosaurs

Insects in fossils

Insect fossils are not often found. Most insects are eaten or fall to pieces before they can turn into fossils. Long ago, the few that fell into mud on the bottom of lakes became fossils. A very few were buried by ash from volcanoes.

Over millions of years this mud and ash became rock. Only the hard parts of the insects remained in the rocks. The thin wings and fine hairs are left as outlines.

By far the best insect fossils are found in a rock called amber. Amber looks like yellow glass. It is made from the **sap** that oozed from pine trees long ago. Millions of years ago, insects fed on this sap. Some were trapped because the sap was sticky. The oldest insects in amber are over 70 million years old.

Survival through the ages

Insects are one of the most successful animal groups. Some of those we see today are very like those that lived long ago. Ants which have been found in amber look just like types living now. Very few other animal types have stayed the same over the ages. Most died out, or became **extinct**, as new types appeared. Such animals could not change with their changing world. One of the secrets of insect success is that they can cope with changes. Most of the insects we see today were already here when humans first appeared on Earth.

▲ The insects in this piece of amber have been there for millions of years. Some types no longer exist, but others have hardly changed. Over half of the types of ant found in amber still exist.

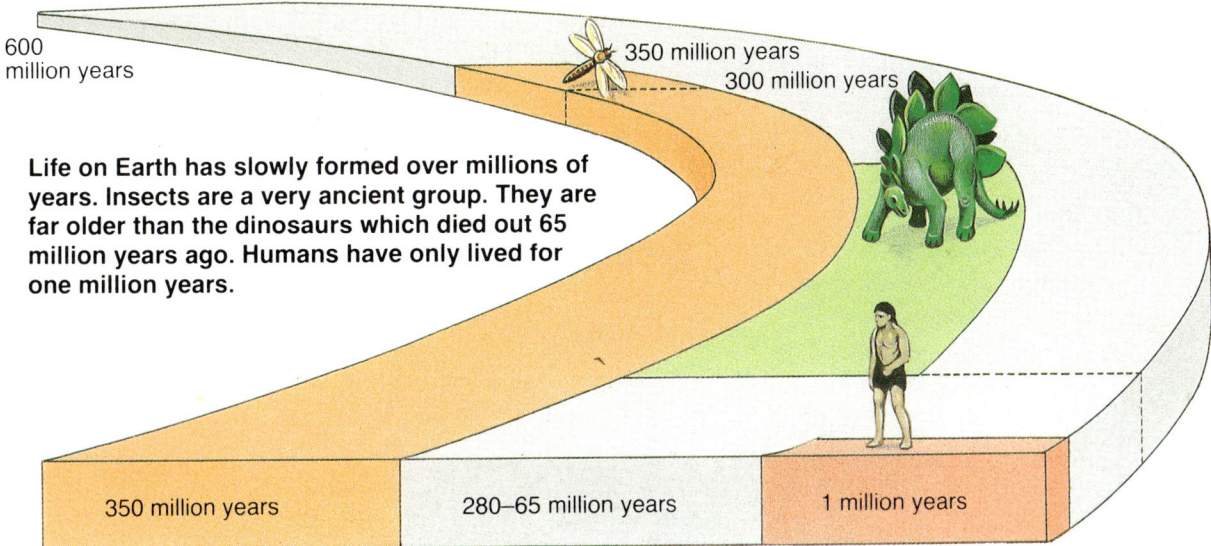

Life on Earth has slowly formed over millions of years. Insects are a very ancient group. They are far older than the dinosaurs which died out 65 million years ago. Humans have only lived for one million years.

9

Thousands of types

There are more different types of insect today than all the other animals put together. Three out of four animals are insects. Almost one million types are known and more are found all the time.

Insects also exist in the greatest numbers. One beehive may have 50 000 bees. Even so, many people do not notice them because they are so small.

Why are there so many different insects? Insects live and feed on plants. There are thousands of different plants. As plants have changed, insects have changed too. They have had to in order to survive. So there are thousands of different insects too.

Insects in groups

Insects are split into groups. There are 30 or so groups called **orders**. An example of an order is the **Lepidoptera** (*lep-e-dop-te-ra*) which includes all butterflies and moths.

Some of the orders contain lots of insects. The beetle order has over 300 000 types. To help sort out smaller groups, each order is then split into families. For instance the stag beetles make up one family.

It is sometimes hard to tell insect types apart. However, each type, or **species**, differs in shape, colour or **habits** from all other insects.

▼ Scientists have found that some types of insects are closely related to each other. They have placed these into groups, a selection of which are shown below.

Wingless insects					
Name	Where they live	Name	Where they live	Name	Where they live
Springtails	In the soil	Bristle-tails	In the soil	Silverfish	In leaves and houses

Winged insects with three life stages			
Name	Where they live	Name	Where they live
Mayflies	The larvae live in water, the adults fly	Grasshoppers and crickets	Among plants
Dragonflies and damselflies	The larvae live in water, the adults fly free	Leaf and stick insects	Among plants
Cockroaches and mantids	Among plants and dead leaves	Booklice	Among dead plants
Termites	In huge nests of soil	True lice	On animals (parasites)
Earwigs	Among plants	Biting lice	On animals (parasites)
Stoneflies	The larvae live in water, the adults fly free	True bugs	On animals, among plants or in water
		Thrips	Among plants

Winged insects with four life stages			
Name	Where they live	Name	Where they live
Alderflies and snakeflies	Among plants and in water	Beetles	Everywhere
		True flies	Everywhere
Lacewings and ant-lions	Among plants and on the ground	Caddis flies	The larvae in water, the adults fly
Scorpion flies	Among plants and in the soil	Butterflies and moths	Among plants
Fleas	On animals (parasites) and in rubbish	Bees, ants and wasps	Among plants and on the ground

Making changes

All insect species live in one kind of place. If food runs out or their living space changes, they must adapt too. If they do not adapt they will die. The simplest change an insect can make is to change its colour.

A colour change happened in a black and white moth called a peppered moth. The pattern of this moth changed in just over 100 years. This was because the tree trunks it rested on became black from factory smoke. These moths like to hide on trees. The wings of the moth changed to black, so it could not be seen easily. This type became more common than the old black and white speckled form.

A more important and faster change happened with insect **pests**. Humans began to use poisons to kill them about 50 years ago. Now these poisons do not work. Insects such as mosquitoes and cockroaches have learnt to resist them.

▲ Not one peppered moth on a tree trunk, but two! A bird would attack the black one. If the tree were black, the speckled one would be eaten.

▼ A male and female mosquito. The male has feathery antennae.

Insect skeletons

The **exoskeleton**, or skin, of an insect is light and strong. It can bend into all sorts of shapes. Insects come in almost any shape you could think of.

A suit of armour

The insect skin is made from a very strong material called **chitin**. It is like a suit of armour. There are many sections which are joined to each other by a thin material which can bend.

Unlike bony skeletons, the exoskeleton cannot grow with the insect. The only way an insect can grow is to shed its old skin and grow a larger new one. This is called **moulting**. It can happen up to ten times in the life of an insect.

When an insect moults, it first grows a new soft skin under the old one. Then the old skin breaks open. The insect pulls itself free of the old skin. Then it has to let the new one dry out and harden.

◀ A whole new skin. A dragonfly moults up to 15 times in its life, getting slightly bigger each time. The old skin still clings to the plant. When the new skin is hard, the dragonfly will fly away.

▼ The middle part of an insect's body. The hard outside skeleton is the frame of the insect. Muscles are fixed to the frame.

Insect skeletons

▲ A close look at a caterpillar eating a cotton plant. Note the segments on the body which let the insect bend.

Many parts

When we look closely at an insect we see that the three main parts each have a different job. The head is used to find and eat food. The **thorax** is the powerhouse. It holds the legs and the wings. The **abdomen** holds all the parts to do with digesting food and laying eggs.

A close look at the abdomen shows us that it is made up of many sections called **segments**. Each segment is jointed to the next. This helps the insect to move the abdomen in all directions. The head and thorax are also made up of segments, but they are difficult to see.

Insect hairs

The outside of an insect's body is covered by tiny hairs. Moths have soft hair which keeps them warm while flying. Some hairs act like tiny fingers which feel the ground. Insects use special hairs to smell or taste. Other tiny hairs tell the insect how damp the air is. Mosquitoes have hairs which act like ears. They can hear the hum of other mosquitoes.

▼ This is the leg of a bee magnified 480 times! The skin of an insect is hard and cannot feel things like our skin does. Instead, thousands of hairs pass messages to the insect's brain.

13

How insects move

Insects move by using their legs or wings. Most types of insects have long legs. These are used to walk or run. Some have specially shaped legs which are used to swim, jump or dig. All insect legs are made up of five main parts. This helps them to bend. Legs always come in pairs. Each pair can look different from the others.

Insect flight

Most insects have two pairs of wings. Some have one pair and a few have no wings at all. Each insect wing has a skeleton of tubes called **veins**. They make the wing strong but light. A thin 'skin' is stretched over the veins. This is made of the same material as the **exoskeleton**.

How does an insect fly? Powerful muscles are fixed to each wing. They make the wings flap up and down. Each wing pushes down on the air beneath. This makes the insect go upwards into the air. Some insects beat their wings very fast. This often makes a humming noise.

Many insects fly very fast. Others, such as butterflies, fly quite slowly. Those with two pairs of wings have the front ones joined to the back ones so they beat together. This helps them to fly better. Insects with one pair of wings fly the fastest. Wings are very important to insects. Flight helps them to escape from their enemies. Flight also helps them to find food quickly. Flying, however, uses lots of energy. This means that insects need lots of food.

Some insects fly thousands of kilometres. This is called **migration**. Some do this to escape the cold winters. Others do it to escape dry weather.

How insects fly. The muscles bunch up in turn to make the wings go up and down.

How insects move

▲ Three pictures taken in under one second help to show how this yellow underwing moth flies.

▶ A pond skater walks on water by spreading its weight on long thin legs.

Insect feet and legs

You can learn a lot about how an insect moves by looking at its legs. If the legs are thin the insect probably runs. If they are fat and hairy the insect might swim.

Those that dig have large front legs which look rather like shovels. Some insects live inside wood. They make their burrows by eating into the wood as they go. They do not have legs, so they move along the tunnels by wriggling.

Some insects, such as fleas or crickets, are terrific leapers. They have very strong legs. The flea is the best jumper in the animal world. If it was as big as a human it could jump over a skyscraper.

15

Seeing and feeling

The insect world is very different to ours. Insects do not see colours or shapes in the same way as we do. Some only see light or dark. Insects do not have noses or tongues as we do. They also have very different ways of tasting and smelling.

Sight

Insects have two types of eyes. Most young insects, called **larvae**, have up to ten small eyes. These are called simple eyes. They tell the insect if it is night or day. Simple eyes cannot see shapes.

Most adult insects have a pair of large eyes called **compound eyes**. Each eye is made up of lots of tiny **lenses**. Each lens can only see part of the view around the insect. By using lots of lenses the insect sees the whole picture.

▲ The compound eye of a peacock butterfly, magnified 75 times. The eye is surrounded by hairs, most of which help to keep the insect warm.

◄ The shaded area shows that insects can see almost all around them without moving.

Compound eyes stick out from the head of the insect. This allows it to see above, behind and below. The lenses of the insect eye cannot move. This means that insects are very poor at judging distances, as they cannot **focus**.

Few animals are able to see in colour, but most insects do. They use colour patterns to recognize their own kind. Each type of insect has its own colour pattern. Insects can see a special colour of light called **ultraviolet**. Many flowers have ultraviolet patterns. Since we cannot see ultraviolet light these patterns are invisible to us.

Seeing and feeling

Feeling, tasting and smelling

Insects are often hairy animals. Some of their hairs serve special purposes. They are used for feeling, tasting and smelling. Very stiff hairs are called bristles. These are often found on the legs of insects. Each time a bristle touches the ground it bends. A tiny **nerve** at the base of the bristle feels this bending and tells the insect where it is safe to walk.

Flying insects have thin hairs on their foreheads which bend in the wind. They tell the insect how fast it is flying. Hairs for smelling are often found on the feelers, or **antennae**. Different types of insect have different shapes of antennae.

Hairs for tasting are usually found on the feet of insects. Flies taste sugar with their feet. Other insects have tasting hairs all over their bodies. Some insects have special patches of hairs which feel warmth. These are used by insects which feed on blood. They can find animals by the heat they produce.

▼ Face to face with a luna moth! The eyes are the two dark patches. The two antennae look like green feathers.

Breathing and feeding

All animals feed to stay alive. Food is turned into energy. To do this animals need to breathe. They take in a gas from the air called **oxygen**. It is used to 'burn' food. Breathing also helps to remove a waste gas, called **carbon dioxide**.

Breathing

Animals such as cows, mice and humans have **lungs**. We breathe by sucking air into our lungs. Our blood system then carries oxygen through the body.

Insects do not have lungs. Instead they have lots of tiny tubes inside their bodies. Each tube connects to the outside air by openings on the side of the insect. These openings are called **spiracles**. From the spiracles each tube branches like a tree. Air taken in moves slowly down these tubes. At their ends oxygen passes into the insect. The waste gas moves into the smallest tubes. It then flows into the main tubes and out of the spiracles.

Many insects live in water. Some breathe by carrying a bubble of air. Others breathe through **gills** like fish do. Water has oxygen mixed in with it. This is sucked across the thin skin of the gills.

▼ Insects have a network of tubes in their bodies which carry air. The air enters the body through tiny holes called spiracles. A spiracle, magnified 200 times, is shown in the lower right hand corner.

Breathing and feeding

▲ A close-up of a tiger beetle's head. Its jaws, at the bottom of the picture, are very strong. The hard pointed tips cut up the insect's food.

Feeding

Insects have mouths like all animals. Most have a pair of sharp jaws called **mandibles**. These are used to cut up plants or flesh. Each mandible has a hard tip. Other insects have different ways of feeding. Bugs have a sucking mouth. Moths have a long coiled tube. A few adult insects do not feed at all.

There are lots of insect types and between them they eat almost anything. Most eat plants or wood. Some eat dung, hair or skin. Many others feed on blood. Usually, each type of insect only eats one type of food. Their mouths are shaped to help them feed. Those which eat plants have sharp, cutting teeth. Blood-suckers have long hollow 'needles'.

Some insects eat many types of food. This lets them live in many kinds of places. Cockroaches and crickets can eat both plants and animals. Their mandibles are broad and strong.

To get energy from food the insect must **digest** it. First, food is taken into the mouth to be crushed. Then it passes along to the stomach. There the goodness is taken out. The useless parts of food are pushed out as droppings.

A life cycle

A **life cycle** is the name we give to the changes that an animal goes through, from egg to adult. There are two kinds of insect life cycles. One has three **stages** and the other has four. The egg, **larva, pupa** and adult are all life stages of insects.

At each stage the insect has a different shape. Eggs are easy to tell from the other stages. The eggs have a tough shell. This keeps the tiny larvae inside safe. Once they have hatched, the larvae grow by changing their skins. An insect usually has four or five sizes of larva. Each one may vary in colour or shape. Insect larvae are given many names. These include grub, **nymph** or caterpillar. The name depends upon the shape of the larvae. Some insects have a resting stage called a pupa. This stage is between the larva and the adult.

The life of a grasshopper

A grasshopper has three stages in its life cycle. It grows from an egg to an adult in a few months. The eggs are laid in sandy soil. Often they stay there all winter. They are protected by a layer of hard foam. The eggs hatch in late spring. The young grasshoppers are called nymphs. Most go through four skin changes.

▼ The life cycle of a grasshopper nas three stages; egg, nymph and adult. The life cycle of a butterfly has four; egg, caterpillar, pupa, adult.

A life cycle

All sizes of nymph look like adults without wings. After the fourth skin change the nymph becomes an adult. The grasshopper never changes its skin again. Adults live up to five months. They spend their lives feeding, mating and laying eggs.

The life of a butterfly

A butterfly's life cycle has four stages. Each cycle takes a full year. Most eggs hatch about ten days after being laid. A few butterflies lay eggs which go through the winter. The butterfly larva is called a caterpillar. Each caterpillar has five skin changes. At each change it may also alter in colour.

Once fully grown, the caterpillar changes into a pupa, or **chrysalis**. After a week or so the pupa breaks open. A perfect butterfly crawls out. It soon unfolds its wings which then have to dry out. Most butterflies only live for a week.

▲ Eggs of a cabbage white butterfly magnified many times. These butterflies lay their eggs on leaves so that when they hatch they have food. The cabbage white has four life stages.

▼ Here we see four honeybee pupae during the pupa stage. The one on the left is the oldest and will soon become an adult.

Insects everywhere

Most insects live on land or in fresh water. A few types live in the sea. Some live in very cold places, others live in hot deserts. Insects are everywhere, from the deepest lakes to the highest mountains.

Where insects live

Most insects live on plants. The largest number of plants are found in forests. Forests in hot countries are very good places for insects to live. A single plant can be home for many different insects. A tree can be home for millions. Some eat flowers, others eat roots or leaves.

At each stage of its life, an insect may live in a different place. Some larvae live inside flat leaves. They are called leaf-miners. The larva of an ant-lion lives in sand. The adult lives in bushes.

▲ The larva of an ant-lion digs a pit in sandy soil. Then it waits, with jaws wide open, for an unlucky insect to tumble into its clever trap.

◄ A dune cricket from the Namib Desert, Africa. The unusual feet stop the insect from sinking into the sand. Note the long antennae and the colouring which helps to camouflage the insect.

Insects everywhere

Insects live in some strange homes. A few types of insects live in caves, in pure darkness. Eyes would be of no use, so they are blind. Others live in salty lakes where no other animals survive.

One of the strangest insects is an African midge. The larvae live in pools which sometimes dry up. Then the larvae shrivel up. The dry midge larvae look like seeds. When the rains return they swell up again and come to life. These larvae can stay dried up for 20 years and still come to life!

Survival of the few

Insects lay lots of eggs. A female housefly can lay up to 2000 eggs. Each egg can grow into an adult in two weeks. If all the eggs that flies lay were to grow into adults, the world could not cope. In three months the world would be covered in a thick layer of flies.

This does not happen, of course. Most eggs or larvae are eaten. Only a few ever survive to breed. Usually there is too little food. Many larvae starve to death. Now and again there is plenty of food. Then the insects quickly spread in huge numbers. Fields can provide lots of food. Many insects become **pests** in fields. Farmers have to kill them to save their crops.

Many insects are eaten by other animals. Some try to hide and escape being eaten. Others are coloured, or **camouflaged**. They try to look like twigs or leaves. A few insects contain poisons. They are brightly coloured to warn other animals. Their poisons help stop them from being eaten.

▼ Insect numbers can multiply at a frightening rate. This tree will soon be stripped bare by the locusts that have landed on it. Locusts are among the most feared pests.

Insect builders

Many insects build their own homes. These help protect them from their enemies. The simplest insect homes are hollow plant stems. Insects often use these to store their food.

Most insects can make silk. Some, like the caddis fly larva, use silk to spin a case. This larva carries its colourful silk case around with it. Some caterpillars spin silk tents, in which they spend the night. During the day they live on the outside, so that they can feed.

Silk is also used to sew leaves together. Many caterpillars live in sewn up leaf rolls. This hides and protects them. A few kinds of ant sew leaves together to make a tent home.

Building materials

Silk is not the only building material. Insects such as ants use twigs and leaves, which they gather into mounds. Other insects make their own 'cement'. They mix mud or soil with their **saliva**. This is then used to make nests or tubes.

The best soil builders are the termites. They are tiny insects but they can build huge nests. Some of their nest mounds reach seven metres in height. Millions of termites live in each nest.

Other insects use wood to build with. Wasps chew up wood into **pulp**. This makes a type of paper. They use this to build their nests.

Bumblebees and honeybees make their own wax. They use this to make perfect **honeycombs** inside a hollow tree or hole.

◀ Weaver ants at work. These amazing creatures fix leaves together to make nests. They use a sticky silk thread produced by their larvae. This glues the leaves together. You can spot a larva being held by one of the ants in the middle of the picture.

Insect builders

Ant city

Many ants build mounds above ground. These are really the roof for the nest. Inside the nest are thousands of ants. Each ant has its own special job to do. Some gather food outside the nest. Others feed the larvae. The success of the whole nest depends on all the ants working together.

The nest contains tunnels with spaces. Each space, or chamber, is used to keep eggs, larvae or food. Each nest has one queen ant. She has her own chamber. Her life is spent producing millions of eggs. These eggs are carried to other chambers by **worker** ants. When the eggs hatch into larvae they are looked after and fed.

◀ It is hard to believe that small insects like termites can build tall mounds like this one in Southern Africa. It is 3.5 m tall.

▼ A network of tunnels joins the chambers of an ant's nest. In one chamber the queen lays her eggs. In others the young are looked after.

Bees and wasps

There are thousands of types of bees and wasps. Most of them live alone. Each builds its own nest burrow in plants or soil. Each nest is filled with food to feed the **larva** once it is hatched.

Wasps and bees use many kinds of food. Some collect **pollen** or **nectar** from flowers, others catch spiders or caterpillars.

Bees are usually very hairy. They can be brown or striped. Wasps do not have hairy bodies. They are often striped black and yellow. All wasps have a very narrow 'waist'.

Living together

Some bees and wasps build huge nests. Each may contain over 40 000 insects. These are called **social** bees or wasps.

Wild honeybees nest in hollow trees. Humans copy this by giving them wooden boxes called hives. Inside the hive the bees build nest **cells** from wax. A queen bee lays an egg in each cell. Each hive only has one queen bee. The eggs hatch into grubs which are fed by bees called **workers**. The worker bees also visit flowers to collect pollen and nectar for food.

▼ A queen honeybee (marked with the red dot) surrounded by some of her workers. They are standing on empty cells into which the queen will lay eggs. The cells have been built by the workers.

Bees and wasps

New nests are formed in summer. The queen bee leaves the old nest with lots of workers. This is called a **swarm**. She leads the swarm to a new hive or tree. Inside the old nest new queen bees hatch out. They leave the nest with male bees called **drones**. Only one queen returns to the old nest after mating. She takes over the egg laying to keep the nest going.

Some of the nest cells are used for food. These are filled with honey which will be eaten by the bees over the winter.

Wasp nests also have a queen. The worker wasps catch other insects for food. They feed these to their larvae. New queen wasps hatch in late summer. They mate and hide away for the winter. All the other wasps die as winter comes.

Jobs for all

All bees or wasps in a nest know what their jobs are. Some are nurses. They feed and care for the larvae. Others clean out rubbish. Many workers fly out in search of food.

The queen keeps the nest together. She produces a special scent or chemical. This is passed from adult to adult in food. This scent stops the workers from trying to lay eggs.

▲ A swarm of honeybees rests while scouts search for a new nest. Buried in this swarm will be a single queen. She has left her old nest because a new queen has hatched there.

▶ Social wasps, or yellow-jackets, on a nest. Eggs and larvae can be seen in the nest cells.

Butterflies and moths

Butterflies and moths belong to the same group of insects. How do they differ? Butterflies usually fly in the day. Moths usually fly at night. Most butterflies are brightly coloured. They have **antennae** with knobs at the tips. Moths are often a brownish colour. Their antennae can be feathery or straight.

Look at the butterfly (above) and the moth (below). Note that the antennae are quite different. The small diagrams show the butterfly and moth at rest. The butterfly rests with its wings closed. The moth rests with wings open.

Avoiding enemies

The wings of butterflies and moths are covered in tiny scales. Lots of scales help to form a pattern on the wings. The scales lie on the wing like tiles on a roof. Each butterfly and moth has a different pattern. Some look like leaves, others match tree bark or rocks. These patterns help them to avoid their enemies.

Butterflies rest with their wings closed over their backs. The leaf patterns are only under the wings. The upper parts of the wings are often brightly coloured. The bright colours help butterflies to recognize their relatives.

Moths rest with their wings held flat. They carry their hiding patterns on the top part of the wings. Moths use scents to find their relatives. Bright colours are no use at night!

Butterflies and moths

▲ A close-up of the wing of a peacock butterfly. The wing is covered in thousands of tiny scales. Rather like the dots on a television screen, the scales join together to form a complete picture, or pattern. Each scale can be a different colour.

A warning in colours

Not all butterflies and moths look like leaves or rocks. Many are brightly coloured in reds, yellows, or blues. Even caterpillars have bright striped coats.

Some moths hide their bright colours. If attacked by a bird they suddenly open their wings. A bright flash of red or yellow scares the bird. Such patterns are called **flash colours**.

Some butterflies and moths have patterns on their wings that look like eyes. These eye spots are there to scare and trick birds.

Many brightly coloured insects are poisonous. Their patterns and colours warn birds of this. Butterflies and moths get their poisons from plants. Birds soon learn not to eat brightly coloured insects.

Not all brightly coloured butterflies are poisonous. Some copy the patterns of other butterflies that are. These copy-cat butterflies are called **mimics**. Birds do not eat them because of their colour. Mimic butterflies must not become too common. If they do then birds might discover their trickery!

▼ The bright colours of this monarch butterfly caterpillar warn birds not to eat it. In nature, bright colours mean poison. Some insects pretend to be poisonous, but this caterpillar really is!

29

Crickets and their relatives

Crickets, grasshoppers and locusts make up one insect group. They all have strong back legs which are used for jumping. Some grasshoppers and locusts can also fly well.

Most crickets eat both plants and animals. They can be found in bushes and on the ground. A small number, called mole-crickets, live in the soil.

Crickets usually have long antennae and small wings. They live in warm parts of the world. House crickets live in houses all over the world.

Grasshoppers and locusts live in fields. They have short antennae and most have long wings over their backs. Those that cannot fly use their wings to glide. All grasshoppers have two pairs of wings. The front ones, which are like leather, cover the thin back ones when at rest.

Grasshoppers and locusts are coloured green or brown to help them hide among plants. Some are coloured dark brown to help them soak up heat from the sun. Once they are warmed up they can jump quickly and fly fast.

▲ A grasshopper feeding on a flower. Its strong back legs are armed with spikes. If attacked, the grasshopper lashes out and jumps away.

Insect musicians

How do grasshoppers and crickets make their well known sounds? Grasshoppers make sounds by rubbing their legs over a tough **vein** on the front wing. A violin makes a sound in the same way. The grasshopper's leg is his bow. The wing vein is the string.

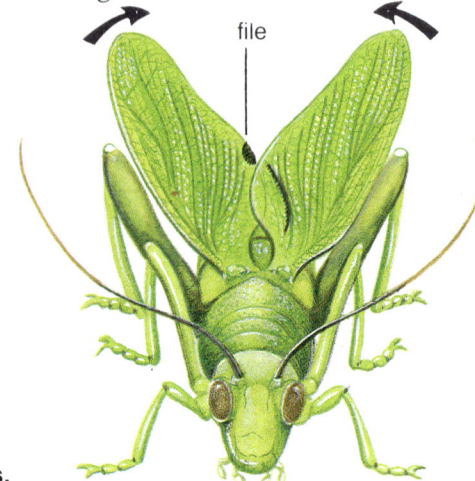

How a grasshopper (left) and cricket (right) make sounds.

Crickets and their relatives

When crickets make sounds they use only their wings. One wing has a thick vein with bumps along it. This is called the **file**. It is rubbed over a tough ridge on the other wing. This produces the cricket chirp. An American cricket has a song that sounds like 'katy-did-she-did'. This has given it the name katydid.

Locusts

Locusts are really just big grasshoppers. Some kinds are found in fields and others live in deserts. They can do lots of damage to crops in warm parts of the world. The desert locust can live alone or in swarms. A single swarm can contain millions of locusts. Swarms appear when there has been plenty of food.

The young locusts are called **hoppers**, because of the way they move. When lots come together we say they band together. Huge bands of hoppers can cover vast areas. They eat everything in their path. When they become adults they fly away in swarms. Each locust is an eating machine. Swarms soon eat themselves out of food. They then starve to death.

▼ Most of us would not be at all happy walking through a swarm of noisy locusts. This man is either brave or quite used to it.

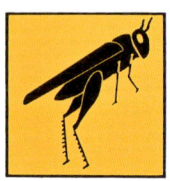

One pair of wings

The name fly is used for many insects. True flies only have one pair of wings. All other insects either have two pairs or none at all. Butterflies and dragonflies are not true flies. They belong to different insect groups.

There are 85 000 different types of true fly. Each uses normal front wings to fly. Instead of back wings they have tiny knobs which look like drumsticks. The knobs are called **halteres** (*halt-hairs*). They help to steady the fly as it flies.

Flies come in all shapes and sizes. The tiniest are a few millimetres long and the largest have wings up to 8 cm across. They are often very bristly. Each fly has its body clearly divided into three parts. The head may have huge eyes. The thorax is square and tough. The abdomen can be quite long and is sometimes brightly coloured.

Many flies have tiny antennae. These can be bristly or end in a knob. All true flies have mouths which suck. Some have short mouths for sucking **nectar**. Others have mouths like needles for feeding on the blood of other animals.

All true flies have four **stages** in their **life cycle** (egg, larva, pupa and adult). Fly larvae are called grubs, or **maggots**, which are usually soft and pale. They have no legs and move by wriggling. Each type of larva is shaped to suit its way of life. Mosquito larvae are hairy. They live just under the surface of the water. Midge larvae look like worms. They live in the mud of ponds. Larvae of hoverflies have strong jaws. They eat greenfly on plants.

▼ Another fly for swatting, or a rather fine creature? The thin wings shine with greens and pinks as this blowfly basks in the sun.

One pair of wings

buffalo gnat

mosquito

hoverfly

midge

horsefly

A few of the many types of fly. All the flies here are adults. All adult flies have one pair of wings. The names of most flies give clues to their habits. For example, a hoverfly can hover and a horsefly bites horses.

The biters

Many kinds of fly bite, to feed on blood. Horseflies are very large biting flies. They buzz loudly and usually bite cows or horses. Tiny flies called buffalo gnats also bite. They are hard to see. American Indians call them 'no-see-ums'. A few biters pass on diseases. Mosquitoes carry a disease called **malaria**. It is a disease which can still kill people in warm parts of the world.

Flies do not sting. Certain types look like wasps or bees, which helps them to fool birds. The flies like wasps, are **mimics**, or good at copying. They even sound like wasps. However, all wasps have two pairs of wings and the wasp-like flies only have one pair.

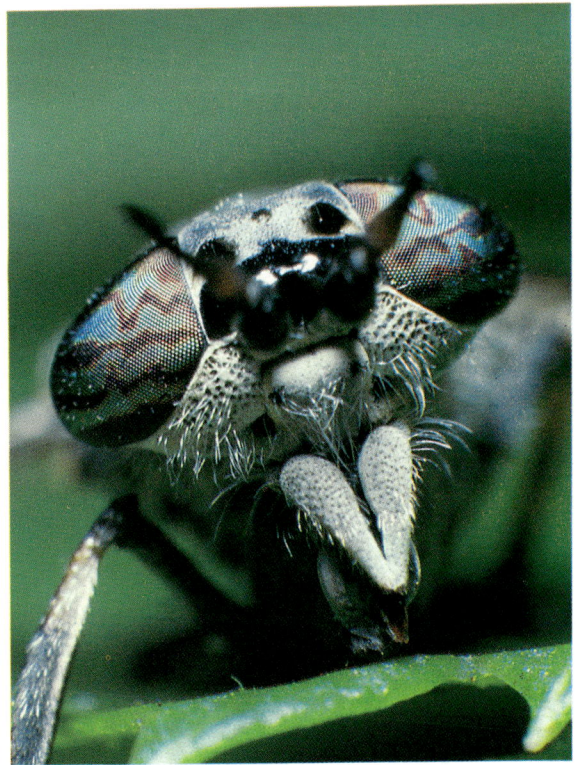

▶ The head of a horsefly, a large biting fly. The enormous eyes take up most of the head. There are 2500 types of horsefly in the world.

33

Bugs and beetles

Many bugs and beetles look alike, but they can be told apart. All bugs have mouths like needles and all beetles have biting mouths.

There are 40 000 types of bug. They mostly feed on plant juices and a few feed on blood. The largest bug is over 10 cm long. It lives in water.

Greenfly and cicadas (*see-car-dars*) are plant bugs. They feed on the sweet **sap** of plants or trees. Another type of plant bug is called a froghopper. Its larvae, called nymphs, live inside a ball of froth. This is often called cuckoo-spit. It hides the larvae from their enemies.

Bedbugs and assassin bugs feed on blood. They bite other animals with their sharp mouths. Some types carry disease.

Meat eaters

Beetles make up the largest insect group. There are over 300 000 types of beetle that come in all shapes. The largest goliath beetles can be 16 cm long. Almost all beetles have very hard front wings. These are no use for flying. These wings cover most of the body. They protect the delicate hind wings which are used for flying.

Most beetles eat plants but some eat other insects. Meat eating beetles have huge jaws. Most meat eaters are called ground beetles. They are usually black and have long legs.

The fiercest meat eaters are the tiger beetles, which are beautifully coloured. The adult has large curved jaws. Tiger beetles can run very fast and most can fly. Their larvae live in holes in flat ground. Each larva sits with its mouth wide open. Its jaws are like spring traps. Passing insects are snapped up as they walk over the hole.

◀ Assassin bugs attack and eat other insects. The prey here is a bee.

Bugs and beetles

Plant eaters

Beetles can eat almost anything. The plant eaters are the most common. The Colorado beetle eats potato leaves and causes lots of damage to crops. Beetles called weevils are also pests.

The larvae of many beetles eat wood. Those of the longhorn beetle bore into trees. Stag beetle larvae eat rotten wood. Some types feed beneath bark or in twigs.

One beetle that does a valuable job is the dung beetle. The adults bury balls of dung. This is used as food by their larvae. Similar beetles feed on dead animals. They are called burying beetles. They bury dead mice and other small animals. Both these types of beetle help clear the world of dead bodies and dung.

▶ Blister beetles are best left alone. If you were to touch these beetles your skin would blister.

▼ A tiger beetle with prey. Tiger beetles move quickly and are good fliers, unlike many other beetles.

Water insects

Many insects live in fresh water. Most prefer ponds or rivers but a few live in fast flowing streams. Water can be a good place to live. It contains lots of small animals and plants which insects eat.

A pond is home for many types of insect. Some, like the pond skater, can walk on the surface. Mosquito larvae hang from the water surface. They have long hairs which spread their weight.

Swimming insects live below the suface. They use their flat, hairy legs as tiny oars. The water boatmen swim upside down. They have a pair of long legs like oars.

The muddy bottom of the pond is home for crawling insects. They also clamber over rocks and water plants.

Most water insects are larvae. Once they become adults they fly above the water. Mayfly and damselfly larvae use **gills** to breathe. Caddisfly larvae usually live inside silk cases. Each case is decorated with stones or sticks.

▼ All sorts of insects can be found in ponds, or on their surface.

Water insects

▲ After becoming adults, dragonflies never return to live in water.

The watery jungle

Underwater insects are often meat eaters. They catch and eat other small water animals. Some, such as the diving beetles, do so by swimming fast. Others use **camouflage** to wait for passing animals.

The water scorpion is a kind of bug. It hides among the weeds. It has a long breathing tube. It uses this to suck air from above the water. The front legs of the water scorpion are used to grab food.

Some insect larvae have sharp jaws. The nymph of the alderfly has huge curved **mandibles**. These snap tight on its food.

Some water insects, like the water boatmen, look silvery. This is because they carry a small bubble of air with them. Many water beetles carry a silver bubble on their 'tails'.

Dragonflies

The dragonfly larva is a very strange creature. It feeds using a very special type of mouth. This is called a mask. The sharp mandibles are fixed to a bent 'arm'. This can be shot out to grab food.

Dragonfly larvae eat many types of animal. They can even catch small fish or tadpoles. They usually move very slowly, but if they are attacked they can escape at great speed. A stream of water can be squirted out of their bodies which shoots them forward.

Once it is fully grown the dragonfly larva leaves the water. It crawls up a plant stem and the winged adult emerges.

Unusual insects

Insects can be called unusual for lots of reasons. They may have strange shapes, or they may live in very strange places. Insects are always trying to avoid being eaten. Many of the more unusual types are good at hiding. Others are unusual because of the way that they protect themselves.

Leaves and sticks

Some of the most unusual insects live in Asia. They are the leaf and stick insects. They do not look like insects until they move.

Leaf insects have very flat, wide bodies. They even have blotches and pieces missing, just like a real leaf. During the day they stay quite still. They feed on leaves at night.

Stick insects can grow very large. An Australian type grows up to 30 cm long. They have long bodies that look like twigs. They are covered in bumps and spines, just like a real twig.

Stick insects are unusual for other reasons. Some types only seem to have females. The males are very rare. The females can lay eggs without mating. Other types pretend to be dead if attacked.

The young of some stick insects look like ants. This protects them from birds. Real ants bite or sting, so the birds stay away.

◀ Stick insects are masters of disguise. They move very slowly to avoid being seen. If one of their legs is broken off they can grow another. Some types can change colour to match their surroundings.

Unusual insects

Living thorns

An insect with a strange shape is the treehopper. Treehoppers are bugs which live in hot jungles. Some can look just like thorns. They even sit along twigs. The treehoppers are green to match real thorns. Others are brightly coloured. Even so, they do not look like insects, until they move. They feed by sucking tree sap. Their good disguise keeps them safe from birds and lizards. Another strange bug is the lantern fly. Its head is very big and hollow. This was once thought to produce light, like a lantern.

Unusual pairs

Male and female insects often look different. Many butterflies have bright coloured males and dull looking females. Some insects, however, have totally different males and females. There are certain female moths that do not have wings. These moths spend their short adult lives laying eggs.

The glow-worm female looks like its larva. The male glow-worm looks like other beetles. It has a hard pair of front wings and can fly.

▲ Disguise yourself as a sharp thorn and no enemy will try to eat you. This group of thornbugs includes nymphs and adults. The adults have larger 'thorns', giving them better camouflage.

▼ These two very different looking insects are in fact male and female vaporer moths. The male is the one with wings.

female

male

Insects in our homes

The houses we live in are homes to many insects. There they find food and shelter. They eat all kinds of things in a house, from left-overs to the house itself.

The types of insects that we find in our homes once lived in warm, dry places. Cockroaches came from hot countries. They were brought to colder countries by the first ships. They climbed aboard the ships without the sailors seeing them, like stowaways!

Other house insects, the clothes moths and silverfish, probably lived in old bird nests. In our houses they found a better, safer place to live. Dead trees once made a home for beetles that live in wood. They now find wooden tables and chairs much warmer homes.

Insects in our homes

Hidden from view

Insects find lots of hiding places in houses. They slip into cracks or below floors. They hide in the roof or under the carpets. We often never know that they are there.

Some only come out to feed at night. Cockroaches like the dark. They disappear if a light is put on.

In the quiet of the night we can hear insect noises. The chirp of the house cricket tells us that it is there. The death-watch beetle makes a tapping sound as its head bangs against its wooden tunnel.

◀ The woodworm, or common furniture beetle, is found in many homes. The floor board shows the holes made by adult beetles. The larvae live inside the wood. They cause the most damage.

▼ Cockroaches feed on bad food and pass on disease to fresh food, like this tomato. So we hate the idea of insects eating our food.

Food in plenty

We do not find many house insects in the wild. The main reason for this is that there is plenty of food for them in our homes. Most houses contain lots of wood. This may be in the floor, in the walls, in the roof, or in tables and chairs. Many types of beetle eat wood. Some types eat so much that they can make a house fall down. They turn the hard wood that supports the house into dust.

Some house insects eat strange foods. Tiny book lice eat the glue which is used to stick books together. One beetle eats tobacco and cigarettes. Some insects even eat dust.

◀ A silverfish feeding on bread crumbs. This wingless insect is covered in silver scales, which makes it look rather like a fish. Silverfish are common house pests. As well as scraps, they eat books and even pictures on the walls.

Insects that cause harm

Insects upset our lives in many ways. They do this by eating our food and buildings, and by spreading disease. Disease can kill humans and animals.

Humans wage constant war against insects. The most common weapons that humans use are chemical poisons. These are called **insecticides**. This means 'insect killers'. Some types of insect become used to these poisons. We say that they become **resistant**.

▶ Cabbage white caterpillars feeding.

▼ This field of potatoes has been attacked by Colorado beetles. Perhaps the farmer forgot to spray this area with insecticide!

Some insecticides, such as one called DDT, also poison other animals. DDT is not used today because of this. Most insecticides also kill insects that help us, like bees. New types of insecticide only kill one kind of insect. In the future they will be used more and more. Do not worry, insects will always survive. They are more successful at living than humans.

Insects that cause harm

▲ A tsetse fly feeding on human blood. They only feed as adults. The females give birth to fully grown larvae, rather than giving birth to eggs. The larvae then change into adults.

Damage to crops

Insects eat everything that humans grow. There are at least 125 types of insect which eat cotton plants. They do vast amounts of damage every year.

Locusts have always been pests. The Ancient Egyptians used to pay people to kill them. Today they still cause damage to our crops. One of the worst pests today is the greenfly. It kills plants by sucking the sap from them. Greenfly also spread disease to plants.

Many insect pests are larvae. The caterpillars of cabbage white butterflies eat cabbages, brussel sprouts, and cauliflowers. Caterpillars of some moths can eat entire forests. Many plants have their roots eaten by insect larvae.

Carrying disease

Some of the most dangerous diseases are spread by insects. Malaria, sleeping sickness and yellow fever are all diseases passed on by insects.

Malaria is spread by female mosquitoes. They feed on blood. When they feed they pass the disease into the body. The disease lives in the blood and quickly spreads.

Sleeping sickness is a dangerous disease in Africa. It is carried by the tsetse (*tet-see*) fly. The female fly feeds on blood. She bites humans and animals.

Stopping the damage

Insecticides are not the only means to stop the damage. Many insects eat other insects. In some countries insects which eat others are put into fields of crops by farmers. This is called **biological control**.

Many insects eat stored foods. This means that much food is lost. Better ways of storing food may stop this damage.

How insects help us

▼ A honeybee hive in an apple orchard. The bees are helping to make sure that a good crop of apples will grow here.

Not all insects eat crops. Some help us to grow them. The insects carry **pollen** on their hairs and feet as they move from flower to flower. Pollen makes a plant produce fruit or seeds. This is called **pollination**. In return the flowers produce **nectar** for the insects. Butterflies, moths, beetles and flies are all good pollinators. They all help our crops and flowers to make seeds. Our best insect friends are the bees. Honeybee hives are put in orchards to pollinate trees.

How insects help us

Clothes and food

Some of the finest clothes are made out of silk. The Chinese have used silk for over 4000 years. Silk is produced by caterpillars of the silkworm moth. These moths are kept on special farms. The silkworms spin a tough case to protect themselves in the **pupa** stage. This is called a **cocoon**. Each cocoon is made from silk thread. The silk thread is taken by humans to make clothes.

The most famous insect food is honey. This is collected from the hives of honeybees. Honey is a mixture of nectar and pollen. The honeybees also produce beeswax, which we use for polishing. Beeswax was once used to make candles.

Insects are eaten as food in some countries. Ants, termites and locusts are eaten in parts of Africa. Grubs and grasshoppers are eaten in some parts of Australia.

▲ It takes about five days for a silk worm to spin its cocoon. This one is complete. The silk is taken before the adult moth can form inside.

◄ Insects can help in the control of plants. Young caterpillars feeding on a prickly pear cactus.

Insect helpers

Many insects help humans by eating pests. The ladybird is the farmer's friend. Their **larvae** and adults eat lots of greenfly.

Insects can be used like tiny grass cutters, to eat weeds. The prickly pear cactus is found in America. Years ago it was taken to Australia, where it became a weed. It spread everywhere, because there was nothing in Australia that would eat it. A tiny moth was brought in from America to eat it. This soon reduced the number of the prickly pear plants.

Perhaps not all insects are so bad! There are many more interesting facts to learn about insects. New insects are being discovered every day.

Glossary

abdomen: the back part of an insect's body. The abdomen is made up of six or more jointed parts
antenna: a feeler on an insect's head. Each insect has two antennae
arthropod: animals which have bodies and legs made of jointed parts. Insects, spiders, crabs and centipedes are all arthropods
biological control: the way that animals are used by humans to keep down the numbers of a pest insect or plant. The animals eat the pest
camouflage: colour patterns or body shapes which help to hide an animal's body in its surroundings
carbon dioxide: a gas found in the air. All animals breathe out carbon dioxide
cell: a very small part, or unit. Beehives are made of hundreds of cells
chitin: a strong material which makes the outside of insects hard
chrysalis: the stage in the life of a butterfly between the caterpillar and the adult butterfly
cocoon: the silken case which protects the pupa of a moth
cold-blooded: describes animals which cannot make their own heat. Their bodies are hot or cold, depending on the weather
compound eye: the large eye of an insect which is made from many parts. Most adult insects have two compound eyes
digest: to break down food inside the stomach and then pass it around the body
drone: a male bee. Unlike the worker bees, drones do not collect honey or pollen
exoskeleton: the hard outer 'skin' of arthropods
extinct: animals which are no longer living, or found on Earth
file: a hard, rough vein on the wing of a grasshopper. The file is scraped over the other wing to make a sound
flash colour: a colour pattern which is normally hidden under the wings. An insect suddenly shows this colour to frighten an enemy
focus: to be able to see something very clearly
fossil: the remains of an animal or plant, usually found in rocks
gill: part of an animal used to breathe under water. Insect gills are often feathery
habit: the usual way in which an animal lives

haltere: the part of a fly shaped like a drumstick. The haltere is used to help the insect to fly straight. It is where the back wing used to be
hibernate: to 'sleep' or stay still through the cold winter. Some insects in hot countries sleep through the dry summers
honeycomb: a layer of wax cells with five sides in which honey bees store their honey
hopper: a young locust
insecticide: a chemical used to kill insects
larva: the second stage of an insect. The larva hatches out of an egg
lens: the clear, glassy part of an eye through which an animal sees
lepidoptera: the insect group which includes butterflies and moths
life cycle: the changes in the life of insects (and other animals) from egg to adult
lung: part of an animal used for breathing air
maggot: a young fly. Maggots have no legs and move by wriggling
malaria: malaria is a disease caused by a very simple, tiny animal. These animals live in the blood of other animals and can kill them
mandible: the jaw or sharp, hard part of an insect's mouthparts. Most insects have two mandibles. Each can be long and curved
migration: the movement of animals from one area to another. These long distance journeys happen at certain times each year
mimic: to look like some other creature or object. Some insects mimic others that bite, or are poisonous
moulting: changing an old skin for a new, larger one. All young insects grow by moulting
nectar: the sweet, sugary liquid that plants produce in their flowers. Many insects visit flowers to feed on nectar
nerve: a tiny 'cable' that carries messages from one part of an animal to another. Most nerves run to the brain
nymph: a young insect. Nymphs look like tiny copies of their parents, but have no wings
order: one of the groups into which insects are split. Beetles belong to one order, flies to another
oxygen: a gas found in the air. Oxygen is very important to all plants and animals. It is used in breathing
pest: an animal or plant which eats something grown, built, or belonging to humans
pollen: the tiny grains, or 'dust', found in flowers
pollination: the way in which pollen is moved from one flower to another to help make seeds. Insects are the most common carriers of pollen

Glossary

pulp: a squashed mixture of wood, or plants, and water. Pulp is used by some insects to build with

pupa: the last stage in the life of some young insects. The pupa is the resting stage when the adult can take shape

resistant: to become used to something. Insects that become resistant are no longer killed by poisons

saliva: a liquid used in the mouth of an animal. Saliva helps to soften food

sap: the watery liquid inside plants or leaves. This contains lots of sugar and other foods

segment: one of the jointed parts that divide up an insect. The bodies, legs and antennae of all insects are divided into segments

skeleton: the hard parts of an animal which give its body some shape. Insects have their skeleton outside the body. Other animals have a bony skeleton inside their body

social bee: a bee which lives in a nest with other bees. Some social bees, such as the honey bee, share the jobs within the nest

species: a group of animals or plants which look alike and can breed with one another. It takes two adults of the same species to produce young

spiracle: one of the tiny breathing holes on the outside of an insect's body. Spiracles are joined to tiny tubes inside the insect's body

stage: a part of the life cycle of an insect. There are either three or four stages

swarm: a large group of bees, ants or wasps. They gather together to move to a new nest or to find mates

thorax: the middle part of an insect's body. The wings and legs are fixed to the thorax. It contains all the muscles to move the wings and legs

ultraviolet: a 'colour' of light which we cannot see. To insects it is a pale type of blue

vein: a long, thin tube which makes up the frame of an insect's wing. Each insect has a different pattern of veins in its wings

warm-blooded: describes animals which can keep their bodies at a steady temperature. They do so by making their own heat. They can lose heat if they get too hot

worker: a special type of female ant or bee that does not lay eggs. Most of the ants or bees we see are workers

Index

abdomen 6, 8, 13, 32
alderfly 37
amber 9
ant 9, 24, 25, 38, 45
antenna 17, 28, 30, 32
ant-lion 22
ant's nest 25
arthropod 6
assassin bug 34

bedbug 34
bee 5, 24, 26, 27, 33
beehive 10, 26, 44
beeswax 45
beetle 10, 34, 35, 37, 41, 44
biological control 43
blood-sucker 19
book lice 41
buffalo gnat 33
bug 19, 34
bumblebee 24
butterfly 10, 14, 21, 28, 29, 32, 39, 44

cabbage white butterfly 43
cactus, prickly pear 45
carbon dioxide 18
caterpillar 20, 21, 24, 26, 29, 43, 45
chitin 12
chrysalis 21
cicada 34
clothes moth 40
cockroach 11, 19, 40
cocoon 45
Colorado beetle 35
compound eye 16
cricket 15, 19, 30, 31

damselfly 36
DDT 42
diving beetle 37

dragonfly 8, 32, 37
drone 27
dung beetle 35

exoskeleton 6, 12, 14
eye spots 29

file 31
first insects 8
flea 15
flash colour 29
fly 32, 33, 44
fossil 8, 9
froghopper 34

glow-worm 39
goliath beetle 34
grasshopper 20, 21, 30, 31, 45
greenfly 32, 34, 43, 45
ground beetle 34
grub 20, 45

haltere 32
honeybee 24, 44, 45
honeycomb 24
hopper 31
horsefly 33
housefly 23
hoverfly 32

insect
  breathing 18
  camouflage 23, 37
  eggs 20, 21, 23, 25, 26
  feeding 19
  feeling 17
  flight 14
  groups 10
  hairs 13, 17
  hibernation 7
  homes 23, 24
  movement 14, 15
  pests 11, 23, 35, 43, 45

sight 16
skeleton 6, 12
skills 5
smell 13, 17
taste 13, 17
insecticide 42, 43

katydid 31

ladybird 45
lantern fly 39
larva 16, 20, 23, 34, 35, 36, 37, 43
  ant 25
  ant-lion 22
  bee 26
  butterfly 21
  caddis fly 24, 36
  damselfly 36
  dragonfly 37
  dung beetle 35
  fly 32
  froghopper 34
  glow-worm 39
  hoverfly 32
  ladybird 45
  mayfly 36
  midge 23, 32
  mosquito 32, 36
  tiger beetle 34
  wasp 26, 27
leaf insect 38
leaf-miner 22
Lepidoptera 10
life cycle 20, 21, 32
locust 30, 31, 43, 45
longhorn beetle 35

maggot 32
malaria 33, 43
mandible 19, 37
mayfly 36
midge 4, 23, 32
migration 14
mimic butterfly 29
mole-cricket 30
mosquito 11, 13, 32, 33, 43
moth 10, 11, 19, 28, 29, 39, 44, 45
moulting 12

nectar 26, 32, 44, 45
nymph 20, 21, 34, 37

oxygen 18

peppered moth 11
pollen 26, 44, 45
pollination 44
pond skater 36
prickly pear cactus 45
pulp 24
pupa 20, 21, 45

queen ant 25
queen bee 26, 27
queen wasp 27

segment 13
silk 5, 24, 45
silkworm moth 45
silverfish 40
sleeping sickness 43
social bee 26
spider 6
spiracle 18
stag beetle 10, 35
stick insect 38
swarm 27, 31
swimming insects 36

termite 5, 24, 45
  food gatherer 5
  nest 24
  nurse 5
  queen 5
  soldier 5
thorax 6, 8, 13, 32
tiger beetle 34
treehopper 39
tsetse fly 43

ultraviolet 16

wasp 24, 26, 27, 33
wasps' nest 27
water boatman 36, 37
water scorpion 37
weevil 35
wing scale 28
woodlouse 6
worker ant 25
worker bee 26, 27
worker wasp 27

48